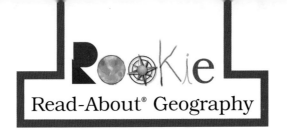

Hawaii

By Christine Taylor-Butler

Subject Consultant
Nanette Napoleon
Cultural Consultant
Kailua, Hawaii

Reading Consultant
Cecilia Minden-Cupp, PhD
Former Director of the Language and Literacy Program
Harvard Graduate School of Education
Cambridge, Massachusetts

Children's Press®
A Division of Scholastic Inc.
New York   Toronto   London   Auckland   Sydney
Mexico City   New Delhi   Hong Kong
Danbury, Connecticut

Designer: Herman Adler
Photo Researcher: Caroline Anderson
The photo on the cover shows a beach off of Kauai, Hawaii.

Library of Congress Cataloging-in-Publication Data

Taylor-Butler, Christine.
  Hawaii / by Christine Taylor-Butler.
    p. cm. — (Rookie read-about geography)
  Includes index.
  ISBN-13: 978-0-531-12571-7 (lib. bdg.)   978-0-531-16812-7 (pbk.)
  ISBN-10: 0-531-12571-8 (lib. bdg.)   0-531-16812-3 (pbk.)
  1. Hawaii—Juvenile literature. 2. Hawaii—Geography—Juvenile
literature. I. Title. II. Series.
  DU623.25.T39 2007
  919.69—dc22   2006017607

CHILDREN'S PRESS, and ROOKIE READ-ABOUT®, and associated
logos are trademarks and/or registered trademarks of Scholastic Library
Publishing. SCHOLASTIC and associated logos are trademarks and/or
registered trademarks of Scholastic Inc.
1 2 3 4 5 6 7 8 9 10 R 16 15 14 13 12 11 10 09 08 07

Do you know why Hawaii is called the Aloha State?

Hawaiian coastline

The people of Hawaii say "Aloha" to greet visitors. In the Hawaiian language, *Aloha* means "hello!"

Hawaii is located in the Pacific Ocean. It is the only state completely surrounded by water.

Can you find Hawaii on this map?

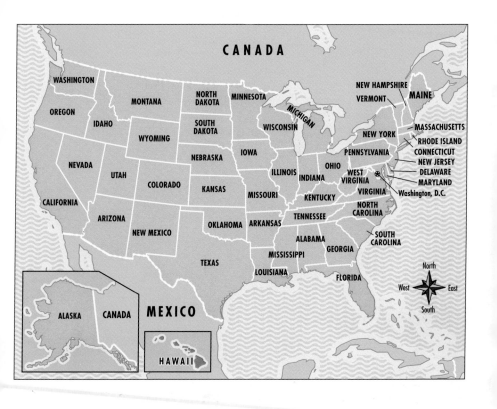

CANADA

WASHINGTON

OREGON

IDAHO

MONTANA

NORTH
DAKOTA

SOUTH
DAKOTA

WYOMING

MINNESOTA

WISCONSIN

MICHIGAN

NEW HAMPSHIRE

VERMONT

MAINE

NEVADA

UTAH

COLORADO

NEBRASKA

IOWA

ILLINOIS

INDIANA

OHIO

NEW YORK

PENNSYLVANIA

WEST
VIRGINIA

MASSACHUSETTS

RHODE ISLAND

CONNECTICUT

NEW JERSEY

DELAWARE

MARYLAND

CALIFORNIA

ARIZONA

NEW MEXICO

KANSAS

OKLAHOMA

MISSOURI

ARKANSAS

KENTUCKY

TENNESSEE

VIRGINIA

Washington, D.C.

NORTH
CAROLINA

TEXAS

MISSISSIPPI

ALABAMA

LOUISIANA

GEORGIA

SOUTH
CAROLINA

FLORIDA

North

West   East

South

ALASKA

CANADA

MEXICO

HAWAII

5

Oahu (oh–AH–hoo) is Hawaii's third-largest island.

Hawaii is made up of
132 islands.

People can live on the
eight largest islands.

Long ago, volcanoes formed
under the Pacific Ocean.
A volcano is an opening in
Earth's surface. Sometimes
volcanoes erupt. Hot, liquid
rock called lava bursts from
the volcanoes' tops.

Each Hawaiian island is the
top of a volcano!

A volcano erupting in Hawaii

One of Hawaii's black sand beaches

Have you heard of Hawaii's black sand beaches?

The sand is made from crushed lava.

Hawaii's largest island is nicknamed The Big Island. It is also called Hawaii, just like the state.

The Big Island is made of the tops of five volcanoes. A few of these volcanoes sometimes still erupt.

A waterfall on Hawaii's Big Island

The top of Mauna Kea

The highest point in
the state of Hawaii
is Mauna Kea (MAO-nah
KAY-ah). Mauna Kea rises
more than 13,000 feet
(4,000 meters)!

Hawaii is the only U.S. state that was once ruled by a king and queen. It became the fiftieth state in 1959.

Hawaii's largest city, Honolulu, is also the state capital.

H A W A I I

OAHU

Honolulu

P A C I F I C   O C E A N

North
West ✦ East
South

Mauna Kea △

HAWAII

SCALE 1 inch = 165 miles

0   Miles   165

0   Kilometers   265

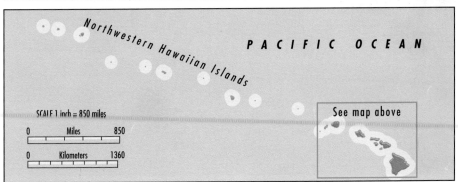

Northwestern Hawaiian Islands

P A C I F I C   O C E A N

See map above

SCALE 1 inch = 850 miles

0   Miles   850

0   Kilometers   1360

Sugarcane plants

Honolulu is on the island of Oahu. Most of Hawaii's people live here.

Farmers on Oahu grow sugarcane and pineapples. Sugarcane is a type of grass. Sugar comes from sugarcane.

Some Hawaiian islands
are made up of grasslands.
Farmers here often
raise cattle.

Other islands are filled
with tall mountains and
steep cliffs.

Horses and cattle on a Hawaiian farm

A yellow hibiscus

Hawaii is known for its tropical rain forests. Thousands of flowers and plants grow in these warm, wet areas.

Hawaii's state flower is the yellow hibiscus (hi-BISS-kuhss).

The state tree is the kukui (coo-coo-EE).

The Northwestern Hawaiian Islands are home to many animals. Some of these animals are not found anywhere else in the world.

Sea turtles, seals, sharks, and many types of birds live here.

Tropical fish and a sea turtle swim off of the Northwestern
Hawaiian Islands.

A visitor to the Northwestern Hawaiian Islands
photographs a bird called an albatross.

In 2006, the U.S. government declared the Northwestern Hawaiian Islands a national monument.

This protects the animals, birds, and fish there from harm by people.

Would you like to visit
Hawaii one day?

Perhaps you'll hike
up a volcano. Maybe
you'll swim in the ocean.
You might even spot
a sea turtle!

Visitors to Hawaii hike along the coast.

Words You Know

cattle

Mauna Kea

Oahu

Pacific Ocean

sea turtle

sugarcane

volcano

yellow hibiscus

31

Index

About the Author

Christine Taylor-Butler is the author of twenty-eight books for children and a native of Ohio. She is a graduate of the Massachusetts Institute of Technology and is also the author of five other books in the Rookie Reader Read-About® Geography series: *Kansas, Missouri, The Missouri River, Ohio,* and *Vermont.*

Photo Credits

Photographs © 2007: Corbis Images: 9, 31 bottom left (Douglas Peebles), 29 (Neil Rabinowitz), 13 (James Randklev), 14, 30 top right (Roger Ressmeyer), 3, 30 bottom right (Dietrich Rose/zefa), 22, 31 bottom right (Royalty-Free), 10 (Karl Weatherly); Dembinsky Photo Assoc./Arnout Hyde, Jr.: cover; Getty Images: 18, 31 top right (Walter Bibikow/Taxi), 6, 30 bottom left (Toyohiro Yamada/Taxi); Kevin Schafer: 26; Superstock, Inc.: 25, 31 top left (age fotostock), 21, 30 top left (Ron Dahlquist).

Maps by Bob Italiano